Babička, Nonna

by christine marie angela

Babička, Nonna

A Collection of Poetry & Prose

by christine marie angela

Dedicated to my family, rodina, la mia familia…

~ That Land Over There ~

What do you know of the land over
there? Across the great divide?

I know the rolling hillsides, the trees bent
deep in thought and memory;
        I know the wounds and the
matrimony of nature and dirt; of broken
earth, and freshly baked bread;

Have you ever tried her cookies? Oh so
sweet! Intoxicating aroma through the
whole house!

But her feet were old and tired, and
they could not,
No, they could not. And so she went.
And all the world, it seems, went, too.

        Sometimes I can smell it still, the
freshly baked bread on the air, and I
know, her light is on somewhere,
        in that land over there.

~ And Her Name Was Anna ~

She was innovative, progressive,
Anachronistic, ahead of her day;
overcoming
a challenging and almost
defeating childhood to become
a "tough cookie," they might say,
And she did indeed love to bake.

But the first woman in a small
town to own her own business;
Transcending her culture,
experience, gender expectations, to
advance far beyond what even she
thought possible; Well beyond
succumbing to abandonment, after her
father died on the train tracks, and her
mother married again;

One night, crouching behind a
shelf, hiding from her stepfather and his
butcher knife, she vowed
To change her story;
She decided,

She would be no tragic heroine,
no sad fireside tale,
Instead she claimed her
inheritance for her own, and became
A budding business woman,
And mother of three, eventually;
Watching each of her children
become the first generation to earn
advanced degrees;

A woman who changed not only
her own history, but the future of all
those to come;
Rewriting her tragedy into victory.
And her name was Anna. Anna
Isabella, if you please.

~ Fridays For Ernest ~

I.

She lit a candle every single
Friday, her whole life;

She'd made a promise, to a
woman, to another Mother, that she
would
light a candle every single Friday,
so that he would live.
And he did. The first child
amongst seven before who hadn't;

After she died, the others tried to
light it for her,
But it just wouldn't
light, no matter how they tried.

Her Promise was fulfilled, they decided.

II.

Ernest tried coal mining, and after
one day, was done.

He was seventeen in nineteen thirteen,
coming alone, by long journey on a
boat, from Italy.
     He didn't have a friend, or
anyone, here.
     Eventually he bought a horse
and carriage;
     And sold produce, a huckster,
used to raising up vegetable gardens in
Melissa, Italy.
     He'd one day pass his green
thumb on down, to his son.
     Then he opened his own store on
Logan Street in the Hill District, where he
met Amelia, who had a strict father.
     So they took a train, and they ran
away, to marry.
     When he opened another store,
near Negley, he gave the stray cats

spaghetti, and was gentle on his customers, when they couldn't pay;

A long train of life came, out of a candle being lit, every Friday.

The days were hard, and long, and the stock crash in '29 brought many to grief, but instead it brought to Ernest, a son.

A long train of life came, out of a candle being lit, every Friday.

My father said, he hadn't known of the horse and carriage until much later.

But he knew about the candle being lit, every Friday,

for Ernest.

~ Rosalie & Esmerelda ~

Once upon a time there was a little girl named Rosalie. Rosalie loved running through the forests with her friends and playing creative games, and sometimes stirring up trouble.

And down in the forest where she loved to roam lived a cranky old woman named Esmerelda, whom the nearby folk called "the old witch."

Esmerelda was a paranoid type, and always worried about the little children stealing from her. She worried about her vegetables, and her cats, and her garden decorations. In turn the little children repaid her worry with constant thievery of these very things, and they developed ever sneakier ways to get a hold of her goods.

One sunny afternoon, when Rosalie was wandering through the woods with her friends, it was collectively decided that a particularly bright-colored, and notably, brand new, garden gnome that Esmerelda had just placed in her garden would sure make an attractive addition to their afternoon games. Rosalie's friends were adamant that they should be able to obtain the gnome easily.

Now Esmerelda, in her ever suspicious state, had placed several booby traps around the property for the prevention of just such an endeavor.

She'd dug holes with her little garden hoe, and covered them up with grass and loose leaves, creating a pit into which a thief might land. Each pit she partly filled in with a pile of sloppy mud, should such a traitor attempt to pass through. Of course, she wasn't mindful that amongst Rosalie's crew, there were a handful of skilled tree-climbers who could see her garden from high up, and could easily spot these traps as she dug them. They could thus design a plan of attack that circumnavigated her intended deception.

The children all knew that as soon as Esmerelda heard a rumbling rustling sound anywhere close to where her booby traps were, that she would instantly come running towards the sound with her broom and beat the living hell out of whomever she found in the mud pit.

They also knew of a particularly nasty old mutt that ran loose in the woods, which just so happened to be mute and could not bark. He could however, still bite and claw as well as any old dog could do.

Baiting the mutt with some of the crop they'd successfully stolen from Esmerelda the afternoon prior (which she was still fuming mad about), they lured the poor beast over to one edge of the old witch's garden, particularly close to one of her special traps. When he was pawsteps away from the pit, they threw in the food, and then ducked out of the way as he dived in after it. Doubling back to the other edge of the garden, where the shiny new garden gnome was shining in the late day sun, they crouched and waited.

Sure enough, old Esmerelda came huffing out of her little house, cursing and wielding her broom like a fierce weapon, waving it wildly around her head. She never bothered to look beneath the leaves and bracken before she started furiously batting that broom at its new inhabitant.

Without waiting to watch her fate, the children rushed in and kidnapped the shiny, bright-colored gnome. Victory was theirs! And hours of fun yet to be had, before the sun sank from the sky.

~ Amalia with an A~

Her strict stepfather may have
kept her from love, were it not for
trains, and for
a great, great, aunt Mary, sharing
stories.

She ran away at 16, certain her
new life as a wife would be an
improvement over residing in a family
boarding house.

They say she loved singing, and
that everyone loved her, clustered
around her dining table, gossiping,
comforting, or telling stories.

She took pride in certain things,
buying good silver, but valued the
simple things, too.

The aroma of baking was always
fresh, and filled the house. There was
never a shortage of food for her guests.

And even when luck grew thin,
warmth could be found at her hearth.

~ To the Snow ~

I.

Apricot shine from the shimmery white,
Glows with a warm fire, a fire from under
rosy cheeks alight in the snow;
  A dancer turns round and round,
arms wild and free, in joy and swirl and
apricot snow.
  Violet intertwined with ivory and
celestial blue from the palette;
  And the dancer dances praise to
the snow and the skies, caught up in the
vibrant pulse, the throb of life;

II.

  Twist and turn around for the
sound of the drum; ice drops from the
chimney;
  A curtain is drawn back by an
unseen hand; A child is taken.

His mother weeps; as an adult he is still her child.

Spirits hang over the place of gathering, and hover over the gathered;

They are drawn closer on this side of the curtain, unable to guess who next may be called away.

Some scars have been covered over by apricot snow. Violet and lavender grace on the hillside; grace cloaked in white snow;

Gentle tears melt with lifedrops the white blanket, covering everything.

A turn in the dance halts the praise of the winter, becomes

A bowed head in gentle grief, turning away from the dance.

A body is blanketed by an unseen hand. In the loss, old scars are uncovered; the body is carried away. To the snow, the dancer falls in tears.

III.

Apricot glow to the shining white cover,
fallen body blanketed in rosy snow;
The lifepulse beats lavender, calling the
fire to light under pale cheeks, behind
closing eyes;
      Apricot snow calls the dancer to
dance again.

IV.

Twist and turn around for the beat of the
drum;
An unseen hand lifts the weight of the
snow; and it swirls to life again;
      A weeping dancer witnesses
        praise to the snow and the skies,
is caught up in the vibrant pulse, the
throb of life.

V.

      A fire glows out from behind
Eyes alight in the snow.

A dancer turns slowly round and
round;
Pointed toe touches the earth
and feels its pulse.
It beats lavender, calling, calling the fire
of the dancer to glow rosy again in the
swirling snow,
And dance praise to the snow and the
skies.
A bowed head in gentle acceptance
and grief lifts with eyes alight in the
snow, turns to dance again;
Becomes part of the vibrant pulse;
The unseen fire beneath the snow.

For my father, who might need all the magic in this story, but who already has the most magical nurse possible...

~ The Magic Nurse ~

She said odd things, Jebedus couldn't help but notice. She was always doing that.

As she bent her plump frame forward, a grey curl escaped her flowery cap.

"Let's see if we can't get a bit more sleep out of these pillows."

"Whatja say?" he muttered at her.

She looked exasperated. "The pillows-- they have to be properly fluffed up in order for the sleep to rub off on your head. Otherwise you won't never get no kinda sleep, love. You should know that." She went on puffing up the pillows under his old mane. "Now, time for the magic bandages."

He grunted, and pulled away.

"Tough patient you are! But I'll git yeh better in no time, mark my words. Now lean sideways will yeh?" She gently affixed the new bandage to his side, explaining, "See, it's the bandage that holds the magic, and that's where all the Get-Better comes in from."

"Rubbish," he muttered grumpily. "You're just an old hag with a heavy hand. Ouch!"

"Best watch what ye be sayin' about me! I ain't no old hag! You know proper well what I am! And if ye know what's good for yeh, you'll roll to the other side real nice-like so I can git the other side magicked up."

He obeyed, begrudgingly. Since the Nurse had come, even he had to admit he'd been getting better, but she was odd. She insisted he write her a letter every night, listing out his remaining symptoms, which she took home with her. Wrapped it in a tight roll and tied it with a red ribbon, she did. Then the roll went into her basket, and off she went home on her bicycle, peddling her old feet down the windy lane.

Each day she came back at promptly eight in the morning, her basket filled once more with fresh medical supplies. On the surface they looked quite ordinary, but there was something decidedly odd about everything she did, everything she said, and everything she handled. There was a warmth in her hands; it was quite unusual for anyone that hadn't just warmed them at the hearth. Especially in such a cold climate. And there was a mischievous crinkle in her smile that made her gap-toothed grin seem pranksterish. She had a magic touch though, all right.

Jebedus found that his wounds inexplicably healed faster than they ever had before, that his energy surged, and that he was even feeling just a little less grumpy than usual, which was usually quite grumpy indeed. She talked a fair deal, but anytime he tried to ask her point-blank what she did that made the magical healing occur, she clammed right up.

"Now don't go getting' smart," she'd say in irritation. "You're my patient and it's my job ter get yeh better, and you don't need to go askin' after my methods." Her tone had a note of finality that implied the conversation was over. Then she'd go right back to her cheery self, buzzing away again about how much progress he was making, and occasionally humming while she worked.

One day while the Nurse was busying herself searching through her basket, he thought he saw the flash of a little green tail swish out of the basket and back inside again – so fast he almost missed it. And so odd, he wondered if his medications weren't making him batty. He figured he'd taunt her a bit.

"What was that?" he asked huskily.

"What was what?" she said cheerily, still turning medical supplies over in her hands, her head in her basket.

"That li'l green thing that done swished its tail at me jus' now."

The Nurse stopped moving. There was silence. Then, "You're mistaken."

But Jebedus pushed the issue. "Sure I'm not. I seen it. Clear as day. Li'l green thing faster than lightening, flicked its tail right out the basket."

The Nurse turned around, very slowly. An odd expression caressed her lined face. "There was nothing," she said, rather forcefully.

"I know what I seen! I may be an invalid but I sure ain't crazy!"

Her demeanor was very calm as she approached the bedside. "Now look here Mr. Jebedus, I ain't never questioned a one of your strange ways.

Only ever took care a' yeh and did me best to make you well. I got to ask you, to let this drop."

Old Jebedus was feeling pretty stubborn, though, and did not want to let it drop. "Is it a lizard?"

Faster than he knew what happened, she waved both hands through the air as if peeling back a heavy curtain, and spread a transparent glimmering shroud all around his head. He suddenly felt very drowsy.

She watched his face closely for a moment. His eyes drooped. He muttered sleepily, "Think I fancy a nap, just now. If that's all right."

She smiled benignly, but with satisfaction. "A nap'll do just fine for now. And when you wake, you'll be feeling much, much better, and all that nonsense talk of lizards and tails will be all but gone from your mind. Sleep, my good man. And sleep well."

And old Jebedus slept well.

When he woke the next morning, he found the sun shining, and his normal aches and pains were nearly gone.

And so was his Nurse.

He called to her, and he peered out the window down the windy lane, where she always promptly peddled her bicycle in right at eight'o'clock. But there was no sign of her.

He fell back in bed with a deep sigh. "Dammit," he said, slapping his forehead.

He began to get out of bed to make his own tea, muttering to himself. "Never ask a woman to reveal her secrets when the shit is working."

~ Sculptures ~

There are not happy endings but
the daily struggle, with its own
tiny victories along the way;
      no epic love story that ends with
a kiss and white horse,
      but there are epic moments,
when time momentarily stops for two
lovers
      to look at each other, and then
the moment passes; But the memory
remains.

      We try so hard to fight the tide, to
dictate to the universe how the wind
should blow,
      as if we know the details and
purposes of that wind well enough to
decide, east or west, hard or gentle;
      as if we had the eyes to see all
things and know all hearts;

There are not guarantees for
love, life, or liberty, but there is breath to
be drawn, like water from a well,
    a purposeful daily struggle, or an
opportunity to
take what's imperfect, rough,
    just a lifeless pile of clay,
    and make
Sculptures.

~ The Monster Upstairs: A Fireside Tale~

Nellis leaned closer to the hearth. Her eldest granddaughter, Cesnie, was curled up on a rug in front of the fireplace, listening.

Her fireside tales were not always sweet, did not always have happy endings, and some were very scary.

Sitting forward in her rocking chair, Nellis cleared her throat, and spoke.

"Our house was old, very old, and huge! Like an old mansion, and four stories high. But the owners had divided it into two units, two floors each. We lived in the upper half, Jed and I, but the downstairs unit sat empty. I often found it left unlocked at night when the landlord was doing repairs. Sometimes I would sneak down and have a look around.

"It was dark and a little scary down there, but blissfully quiet. The whole place was bare, carpeted but without furniture. It was very clean. There were no puppy scratch marks on that fireplace like there were on ours. There was no spackle-patched hole in the bedroom wall, like the one Jed's fist had left in ours. I knew *he* wouldn't go down there, wouldn't leave the droning comfort of the TV screen."

She paused, adjusting her shawl. "He wasn't always a monster, that Jed. In the beginning, sweet enough. But sometimes he'd wake suddenly in the middle of the night, punching the pillows and yelling, '*Fuck!*' I don't know what he dreamt about, but it would make me shake awake, terrified."

Cesnie's eyes widened to hear her grandmother curse, but she remained silent, listening intently.

"That downstairs apartment was so peaceful in contrast. On this particular night, I'd escaped down there after a big fight with Jed. He'd insisted we watch TV together. I gave in to keep the peace, which I did too often in those days. You wouldn't think me so submissive now," she said with a wink at Cesnie.

"No gramma, no one I know would ever mess with you!"

Nellis smiled gently at her grandchild. "But he was like a loose wire and you never knew when it would spark. Suddenly he was towering over me, yelling and causing the whole house to shake while I shrank under his six-foot-five frame." She paused, and rocked for a moment in her chair before continuing. Her gaze was far off, as though she was reliving the awful scene.

"We ended up in the kitchen, where I was cornered. Then, somehow I wriggled away, and escaped towards the front door. I had to run out the door without even a cell phone or keys. I had nowhere to go."

She paused again and looked down at Cesnie, whose eyes were

round and huge; she was hanging on to every word.

"So I found myself hiding out, ridiculously, in the abandoned apartment downstairs. I stayed down there for a good, long while. I walked through the huge, empty rooms, fantasizing, imagining what it would be like to live there instead. Alone at last, in quiet. A safe place, where the monster was only upstairs..."

Nellis lapsed into a reflective silence, which Cesnie interrupted impatiently.

"So did you stay down there the whole night? Or did you run back upstairs and grab the doggies and take them away somewhere? Did you run away from him that night?"

Nellis sighed deeply. "No."

"Then did you sneak up behind him and push him down the steps, or beat him over the head in his sleep?"

"No." Nellis eyed her granddaughter carefully. "This is not a movie, Cesnie. This was real life."

Cesnie looked puzzled. "But he— you said..."

"Understand dear, that I am a woman of great practicality. The apartment belonged to me, everything inside of it, mine. Running away wasn't an option. And hurting him hardly was either. I wasn't going to go to jail for him!"

She paused, her expression filled with distaste. "I was scared, yes. But I went back home that night. I let him make up with me. Let him cajole and apologize, and promise to change, as he always did. But from that night on, I knew that *I* had to change. And that I had to be cunning."

"So what did you do, gramma?" Cesnie was sitting bolt upright now, staring wide-eyed at her grandmother.

"I packed in secret. Late at night. When he was asleep, or out at the bar. One box at a time. First I packed the items on the shelves that meant the most to me – the family treasures and the books; then I filled in those the empty spaces on the shelves with the things I didn't care about."

Nellis chuckled softly. "He never noticed. He was a blind fool. I did the same thing with my clothes. Told him I was redecorating, was buying new furniture for us, needed to get rid of the old stuff, so I got my favorite couches and chairs out. Right into storage. I left the furniture that was pock-marked with his cigarette burns and alcohol spills because I didn't want it anyway. Then I contacted my landlord and prepared to terminate the lease."

"And he never suspected?"

"No. I went on giving in to all of his demands. I played the role. To protect us all. I led a double life. And that was around the time I met your grandfather. Understand, I wasn't looking for love. I was just trying to escape unscathed."

"Did you?"

"Nearly. A few days before the lease was due to end, I told him that I could no longer afford the place. Said I was going to stay with family. That he could stay but would have to sign a new lease with the landlord. He was boiling mad, but smart enough to know he was against a wall. There was nothing to keep the landlord from calling the police if he wouldn't leave after I was gone. And so I escaped."

Cesnie stared at her grandma in disbelief, as if seeing her as a person for the first time. As a woman for the first time.

"Wow, grandma. You were really brave to do all that. Weren't you scared of him reacting bad?"

"Yes."

Then she looked hard at her granddaughter. "But not as scared as I was of staying. Of giving myself up to be a slave to someone else. And living in the prison he'd made for me."

"Geez." Cesnie shook her head. "That's crazy."

"Yes, it was. Maybe now you can understand why your mother and I try to teach you how a man *should* treat a woman. So you have higher standards for yourself, and will not get entangled like that, with a monster."

Cesnie leaned back, gazing into the fireplace, transfixed by the warm blaze.

She was deep in thought for several minutes, reflecting on her grandmother's fireside tale.

Finally she said slowly, "If you hadn't done all that, and run away to that downstairs apartment, and imagined your life being different that night, you might still be living there, with him. You never would have met Grandpa Jim, and I might not have ever come along at all."

She paused. "That one choice, that night, changed the course of your whole life."

Nellis smiled, pleased. Cesnie was young, but very bright. She had understood.

From upstairs, the sound of Grandpa Jim's gentle snoring could be heard through the floor. Nellis smiled again, and leaned back in her rocking chair.

Except for the quiet crackle at the hearth, the house was quiet. There was no monster now, upstairs, or anywhere near.

~ Story ~

The airport bar was busy. Strangers bustled and they hustled, and they drank, and watched each other warily, or at turns, lustily, from their perch. Matthew arrived alone. His head ached and he wanted quiet.

"Table in the back, please," he mumbled to the hostess. She smiled a lovely, sweet, teeth-whitened smile that was fake and faded from her face as soon as she turned on her heel.

As he was guided him through the airport bar, he passed an older couple, grayed and bent, the woman holding her husband by the hand. The man looked thin and wan, but he smiled happily at her as she held his hand. Matthew was attractive, young and spiritely but he envied this man. He could see plainly that the woman would never leave his side, no matter what trial he went through. He knew he'd never get that from his own wife. She'd rather be bothered with her card games and friends than with their marriage, or him.

Sliding into the booth he was led to, he immediately grabbed the wine list. "Merlot," he said, never lifting his eyes to see the waitress. Once his drink was in hand, he turned his attention turned to the rumpled spiral bound notebook that he'd set down next to his wine glass. He really needed to accomplish some writing.

Almost as soon as he began to think about the task ahead of him, he felt depressed. The din of bar chatter was farther away and the lighting was dimmer back here. He peeled the notebook to a fresh page and uncapped his pen expectantly.

Nothing. Again. Still.

Sighing, he leaned back and sipped his wine slowly. Trying to savor it. The way he never managed to do with anything at all. The lights seemed to dim even more.

He frowned, glancing at his watch. It was only 7pm, surely they wouldn't close for hours.

The lights dimmed further and he tried not to feel alarmed. He didn't remember passing anyone who looked like a terrorist, he reassured himself.

Suddenly a "whoosh" like a strong breeze whipped through his section, swished past his head, and seemed to settle at the next table. It had grown very dark he observed, and the space around him had become almost impalpable. Something stirred, and the lights seemed dim impossibly even more than they were already.   A buzzing sound filled his ears and when he blinked, something like an invisible whitish flame blazed to life in the next booth over.   It did not have a face but was surely male, a presence he could not personify, but could not deny.

"What? Who? Ok... I'm going mad. But...what are you?" he said tensely.

The presence flickered. "I am Story."

Matthew just blinked at it. "So. Ok. Let's pretend for a moment that I'm not going mad and that you are real, and that I haven't had a shitload of wine already today, at the last bar. So, what, are you like, the god of Stories then? Come to inspire me? A muse? Or Apollo, or some nutzo angel of death, or...what?"

The invisible flame moved slightly but made no sound. Then the voice said, "I am no god of anything, nor am I named in any way you described. However, I am Story."

Matthew shifted uncomfortably in his booth. "So are you like some ghost of Christmas past? Present? Future? Have you come to reveal my destiny?" He chuckled derisively.

A hoarse whispery laugh emanated from the creature. "No. I am Story. And you, are a Story Teller. You must write me."

Matthew rolled his eyes. "Oh, for the love. Are you serious? Ok who put you up to this? Is this some kind of sick joke? From someone who knows I have a writing block?"

The creature made no reply but remained still. It didn't look like something anyone he knew could conjure up, Matthew realized. This looked real.   He wondered if his wife was trying to make him think he was nuts so she could control him even more.

Then he realized that no matter how much his logical mind sincerely wanted to deny the likelihood of a creature named Story, some tiny, irresistible part of him wanted to believe in it. The same part that manages to convince a man that the beautiful woman he just met might really fall for him in return, and that she'd be perfect, and really manifest the lovely qualities she displayed upon their first meeting forever. The same part of him that believed his sports team could somehow resurface in a game where they were down 20-zip in the final quarter. That part. The impossible part. The part that still believes in love, and chivalry, and wonderful things.

For a moment, he believed. Then the moment was gone, and he was just an ordinary, cynical man again, who understood that women and sports teams will always let you down, and that invisible things just don't exist.

The creature seemed to sigh, a loud and mournful sound, and began to dissipate. Its presence had held promise, opportunity, a horizon of possibilities that might now never be realized.

Matthew paid his tab, and gathered up his scattered nerves, and strode out of the restaurant towards his gate.

On the way, he passed the same old couple he'd seen coming in. There was no mysterious aura around them, no wealth of mysticism and unknown, as he'd tasted in the airport bar. But they held hands, somehow still smiling, and he saw that the man wore an oxygen tube.

He'd have expected them to look miserable, but they looked happy, the kind of happy that isn't roses and sunshine and happy endings, but might be hospital beds and medication, and tears. But they were both smiling, and he realized, the presence had left him because he'd tried too hard to chase it.

The Story had been there, all along, all around him, he'd just been too foolish to see it properly.

He dashed off to his gate, yanking his pen and notebook out as he ran. If he hurried, he might just have enough time to capture it before it was too late.

~ the wake ~

I know I can offer her no comfort,
She does not know my name;
    She doesn't recognize my face,
or understand why I stand in front of her
now;
    She keeps asking about Fairmont
Street, where she used to live;
No one here is actually crying because
they know they are celebrating a long
life;
    I'm wondering what it feels like to
live to be ninety-four; is it harder to say
goodbye to a life lived that many
years? Or do we accept death more as
we age?
    She has alzheimer's and I know, I
can offer her no comfort, but the
women, they try to tell her: That's your
sister, there, that's your sister.
    She doesn't seem to understand.
She goes over to the woman, lying so
still.
"Is this my sister? My sister?"

I think maybe she understands. They show her a picture, point to Theresa, and to Jilda; This is your sister.

The women are crying now. My eyes tear. She begins to cry now, too. I think she is starting to understand. That's her sister, lying there.

When I was only this big (they're all saying, we remember when you were only this big), and they marveled at the baby girl, and googooed over me; I never dreamt, then, that this might be a little of what life is like; I didn't know, back then, about death.

A man gets her coat while the women hold her; There is love here, I think she understands.
I go off with my family for dinner sandwiches, our comfort, our tradition. We eat when someone dies.

It isn't all sweet, but there's something in the hurt where the love comes in, and the comfort I cannot give comes to her from somewhere, I cannot quite say, but I know it's there.

~ aunt mary's clock ~

Standing under an antique, unpolished
clock that's stopped
at exactly the wrong time;
in a new place, the physical space to
define this metaphysical crossroads;
or, perhaps, the time is exactly right?

i may have used the wine to turn a few
glasses into frogs, and princes into
water; But now it's time to decide.
To my left is a rocky uphill climb, a
glance behind reveals rough terrain;
To my right an easier route, a forgiving,
flat landscape;

The silly clock always stops; it has hung
over the mantle at Duncan Street,
against the red brick on Liberty Avenue,
atop the Amish fireplace on Troy Hill,
and now, here. Over all my comings
and goings, my poorly chosen guests,
and nights alone as well.

As each path turns, I've occasionally stumbled, unsure how to follow the road when it curves sideways;

The swaying dandelions of decision wave in the distance before me, nodding their petals knowingly. They already know what I've decided; it's uncanny.

The clock, stopped, again; After all, just a representation of measurement, of man made time – an illusion. But there are moments, connections, memories, spaces in the universe where souls collide, maybe for five minutes, or for fifty years; they'll decide, in the space of a series of heartbeats.

Every decision, that swaying dandelion in the breeze; left or right, forward or stand still?

Sometimes you make a choice and creation materializes;

Suddenly the realm of infinite possibilities unfolds into one reality;

like a deck of cards falling down into one;
like dice hitting the floor;

surrendering all that was to allow for what will Be;

Motion, emotion, energy, transition, possibility;
A decision is made, and an old clock, once again, begins ticking.

~ Stages of Change ~

I speak to my mother, about
The stages of change
As we drive in her
Black vibe to the mall.

We talk about my clients and the
struggle of being torn between the
desire to get high, and the increasing
understanding that it's destroying them;

I can tell them everything I know,
and it's not enough, but losing a child,
or spending the night outside, might be.

Sometimes we all progress rather
slowly,

here, on this continuum of
change,

but with two steps forward for
every step back.

~ The Old Tree ~

Blood, bone, genetic coding, memory;
What exactly, is family?
Dinner, wine, and story telling,
Gathered around the table, maybe for
hours;
Or,
a language, a song, a letter, a
photograph, a shoulder;
A story to tell, a ride to work?
A reason to begin life,
and companions when we leave it
behind, for more distant shores.
Or
An enormous tree: oak, birch, hawthorn,
willow; with roots embedded deep in
the soil,
Keeping us tied to the earth, grounded,
a starting point, before we climb the
branches
to fly away and return,
perhaps
again and again.

~ Draft ~

      I said, I finished my
Master's thesis, finally, but
it was just
a draft.
      Just a draft, so it's not altogether
too perfect, yet,
there's still editing to do.

My dad said, "That's ok, Christine,
      most of life is
      just a draft."